BERMUDA

Macmillan Education
Between Towns Road, Oxford, OX4 3PP
A division of Macmillan Publishers Limited
Companies and representatives throughout the world

www.macmillan-caribbean.com

ISBN: 978-1-4050-9487-0

Design by Alison Forde
Typeset by J & D Glover Ltd
Cover design by Alison Forde
Maps by Peter Harper

The authors would like to thank the following:
Harriet Zois and the team at Lou Hammond & Associates, Joy
Sticca and the Bermuda Department of Tourism, Bermuda National
Trust, Vince Caan, David A. Woodhouse and Waterloo House, Pink
Beach Club, Elbow Beach Bermuda, Alan Trew and the Fairmont
Southampton, Bermuda Underwater Exploration Institute, Reef
Explorer, 9 Beaches and Duncan Card.

Printed and bound in Malaysia

2012 2011   2010   2009 2008
10 9 8 7 6 5 4 3 2 1

BERMUDA

Photographs by Donald Nausbaum
Text by Madeleine Greey

MACMILLAN
CARIBBEAN

contents

introduction

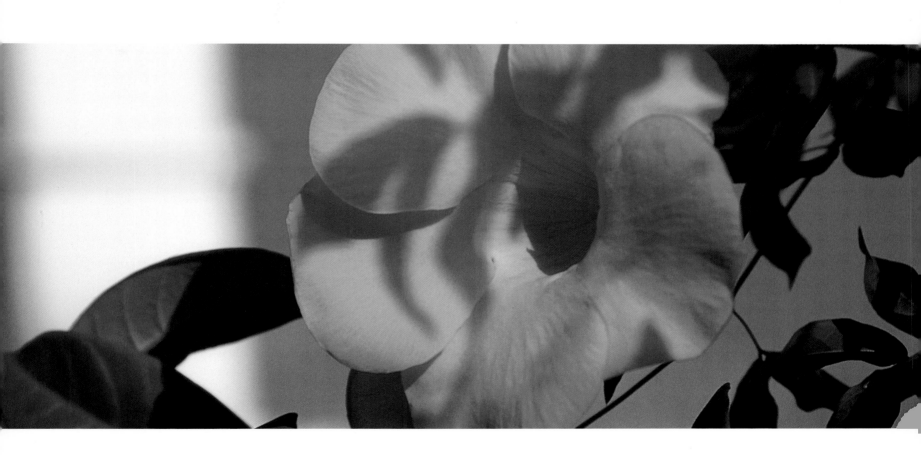

Bermudians are accustomed to being misunderstood. According to popular belief they live on an island in the Caribbean, yet Bermuda is actually a chain of green islands in the North Atlantic.

Gleaming yachts bobbing in the harbour, wide sand beaches and world-class golf courses have given it a reputation as a playground for well-heeled tourists, yet the economy runs on international finance. The hot, humid wind rustles through palmetto and date palm fronds, stirring the air into a frenzied perfume of frangipani, hibiscus and calla lily. Narrow roads wind past manicured parishes, the houses laughing out loud in a palette of childhood colours. This idyllic scene is reflected in the island's impossibly clear, turquoise waters. Bermuda may seem familiar from afar, but once you arrive there's no place like it.

Geography has bestowed both gifts and challenges upon this tiny nation, just 22 miles (35 km) long and 2 miles (3 km) across at its widest part. For centuries it stood vacant and untouched by humans, owing to its remote location. It was only discovered when a hurricane blew a British ship called the *Sea Venture* into the reefs that form a forbidding ring around the island chain. The year was 1609, and British Admiral Sir George Somers was bringing settlers and supplies to the fledgling colony of Jamestown, Virginia. After a new vessel was built and the ship continued on its way, some settlers remained behind. The chance discovery forged a relationship with Britain and America that continues today. In fact, it's difficult to know which country influences Bermuda's culture more.

Of course, in law and government, Bermuda is more British than anything else. It became Britain's first colony in 1684. Today, it's known as a British Overseas Territory, one of 14 under UK sovereignty, yet it's completely self-governing.

Proximity tells another tale. While England lies more than 3,000 miles (4,800 km) away, only 570 miles (917 km) separate Bermuda and North Carolina. For centuries after the first colonists ran aground on its shoals, the locals became increasingly entangled in the affairs of their neighbour to the west. During the American War of Independence and the US Civil War, Bermuda's British loyalties were tested, but business prevailed. In 1775, Bermudians managed covertly to supply George Washington's rebels with gunpowder in a bid to remove a Continental Congress embargo that had halted the vital flow of grain to the island. A century later, in 1861, they made a fortune ferrying supplies and ammunitions

Hamilton is a blend of high-powered business and genteel tourism.

to the Confederates. Only an island far from the motherland could get away with such chicanery … and profit from it.

Revenues have continued to soar in Bermuda, especially in the past 20 years. As an offshore financial centre, this tiny island chain is one of the world's most important business centres. More than 10,000 international companies are registered in Bermuda and over 750 of the Fortune 1000 companies have subsidiaries here. It's a global leader in insurance and re-insurance. Limited taxation may be the draw, but Bermuda's reputation and highly developed infrastructure clinch the deal. Although only four (albeit huge) banks are licensed in Bermuda, the system enables the country's tightly controlled regulatory system to operate more efficiently, preventing money laundering and other illegal activities.

The hub of this rich island is Hamilton, a city of only 1,800 residents that swells into a well-oiled machine of some 14,000 from Monday to Friday. Incredibly, Hamilton takes up fewer than 200 acres (making it one of the world's smallest cities), but it generates about $3 billion a year towards

Bermuda's gross domestic product. All this in a seaside town that certainly doesn't look like Wall Street with its quaint row of low, pastel-hued shops lining Front Street.

Hamilton is a blend of high-powered business and genteel tourism. During the height of the summer season, a policeman dutifully climbs into the old Birdcage pedestal at the intersection of Queen and Front to direct traffic, overseeing a steady flow of rushing mopeds, taxis, cars and vans interspersed with languid horse-drawn carriages ferrying perspiring visitors in baseball caps. Mammoth cruise ships berth along Front Street, casting cool shade and refuge from the beating sun. Every garden, every window box is meticulously manicured, with vast, putting-green carpets of grass stretching from government buildings and commercial highrises.

Weekday lunch hour brings a cacophony of hungry office workers speaking a worldly mix into cell phones and BlackBerries. English accents from America, Canada and Britain are easier to pinpoint than the elusive Bermudian lilt. Busy it is, but not chaotic, for the locals adhere to strict regulations. Signs at the entrance

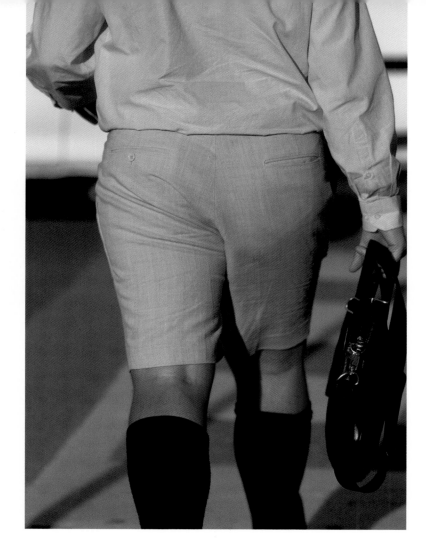

to office buildings caution: 'No helmets, please', while the writing on the pavement nearby forbids scooters. Is there another island in the world that won't let tourists rent a car? Or that prohibits men from riding shirtless on mopeds or scooters? Only one car is allowed per residence, with the exception of doctors, and the national dress code for men has become iconic.

If you're a fan of Bermuda shorts, April to November is prime viewing time in Hamilton. Bare knees are exposed daily as both natives and expats conduct business in the city, dutifully abiding by the strict, three-inch-above-the-knee decorum. While tailored blazers, crisp Oxford button-ups and smart ties complete the ensemble, the range of colours for one's shorts appears boundless. Newly arrived businessmen are likely to opt for discreet grey and black, while veterans don shorts in splashy turquoise, lime green or salmon pink. Bermuda hose (long, knee-high socks) are de rigueur, as are a pair of snappy loafers with tassels. The shorts were apparently the invention of British soldiers stationed in India who chopped off half their trouser legs to survive the searing heat. Hamilton is now considered the best place in the world to buy these practical garments, and Irish linen is deemed the material of choice.

More opportunities for gawking arise at Sessions House, home of the Bermuda Assembly and Supreme Court, both open to the public and both thoroughly British – the justices are resplendent in royal red robes and white wigs. Nearby is the Cabinet House, built in 1833, where the premier and his cabinet have offices. Sessions here can also be observed.

Bermuda's first postmaster, William B. Perot, was a true innovator. Appointed in 1821, he had already acted as unofficial letter carrier for years, greeting ships in Hamilton Harbour and tucking letters under his hat to deliver around town. By 1848, Perot was hand-printing his own stamps, placing Bermuda squarely on the philatelic map – it was the second country to

If you're a fan of Bermuda shorts, April to November is prime viewing time in Hamilton.

Bermuda is not a single island but an archipelago of disputed number.

produce a British colonial postage stamp (Mauritius was the first). Perot's endearing history is highlighted at the charmingly neat and sparsely furnished Perot Post Office in Hamilton.

Within walking distance is Waterloo House, one of the island's finest boutique hotels. The main building, an elegant manor house circa 1815, is the gateway to a 2-acre haven perched on the edge of Hamilton Harbour. Every room is luxuriously appointed with antiques, French chintz, period furnishings and original paintings. These days, management is also proud of its wireless Internet connection. Many of the hotel's guests come for business, and regulars leave their luggage behind to be laundered and stored until their next visit. After all, where else would you need Bermuda shorts and knee socks? Those not travelling on business are free to enjoy the hotel's serene ambience.

Towering above Waterloo House is Fort Hamilton, situated on a hilltop on the outskirts of the city. It's just one of a hundred forts standing sentinel across Bermuda that offer a connect-

the-dots visual history of the island's conquests, conflicts and insecurities. This pentagonal fort, replete with canons, gun emplacements and ramparts, was constructed in the 1870s to defend Bermuda against a possible attack by American forces. But it's the landscaping initiated in the 1960s that makes it particularly interesting. Surrounding the fort is a dry moat 30 feet (9 metres) wide that was once a dumping ground. Today, it spills forth with a dramatic representation of Bermudian flora. A pathway meanders through a verdant alley of soaring bamboo draped in eerie strands of grey Spanish moss, punctuated by shaggy mop palmettos and the fans of traveller's palms. In contrast, the fort's lawn above is a thick carpet of meticulously tended grass, where weddings and cocktail parties convene to take in one of the most spectacular views of Hamilton, its harbour and nearby Paget Parish.

Bermuda is divided into nine different parishes or counties. You can travel from one end to the other in just over an hour (at the island-wide speed limit of 21 mph/35 kph) and the locals like to boast that they're never more than a

'You die and go to heaven, I'll stay here in Bermuda.'

mile from the coast. Bermuda is not a single island but an archipelago of disputed number, since dozens of the original 173 islands and islets have been blasted, merged or absorbed into military bases. The mainland consists of six principal islands, and visitors often don't know they're moving from one island to another until they arrive at the causeway.

The bulk of the outlying islands are uninhabited, but all are named, from Agar's to Zeta. Several are now nature reserves, the most important being Nonsuch Island, where nests of Bermuda's national bird, the cahow, are protected dearly. This bird has a remarkable history, given that it was considered extinct for 300 years, and rediscovered in 1951. Nocturnal seabirds, cahows were so prolific on the island when the first colonists arrived that they dubbed Bermuda 'Isle of Devils', frightened as they were by the night-time screeches of these ghost-like birds.

A handful of Bermuda's outlying islands are privately owned. German billionaire Curt Engelhorn resides at Five Star Island while Bermudian e-commerce king James Martin calls

Agar's Island home. Name-dropping is a national sport here and has been for decades. Mark Twain brought fame to the islands with his oft-quoted line: 'You die and go to heaven, I'll stay here in Bermuda.' America's rich and famous (artist Winslow Homer, Charlie Chaplin and Woodrow Wilson, to name a few) have followed in his footsteps. Currently, former presidential candidate Ross Perot, New York mayor Michael R. Bloomberg and former Italian Prime Minister Silvio Berlusconi all own a coveted piece of Bermudian real estate.

Johnny Barnes, meanwhile, is one local figure whose bank account has nothing to do with his notoriety. For more than 20 years, Barnes has stood at the Crow Lane roundabout outside Hamilton in the early morning hours, spreading his own special mixture of love and good will. Wearing his signature straw hat and broad smile, Barnes stands with arms outstretched, calling out 'I love you, I love you!' to rush-hour commuters. He elicits honks, smiles and sometimes shaking heads but it's front page news when he doesn't show up on sick days. 'Bermuda's friendliest man' has been immortalized

Bermuda's unique climate, both under and above water, is a direct result of the Gulf Stream, which brings warm water into the region, warming the air and affecting Bermuda's flora and fauna.

in a bronze statue near the roundabout. When tourists stop to speak with Barnes, he offers a postcard of himself for a dollar.

Not far from the statue is the Bermuda Underwater Exploration Institute, where visitors can check out one of Bermuda's finest collections of marine artifacts and an astonishingly beautiful display of thousands of shells collected from around the world. A life-size replica of a fearsome 500-pound (225-kg) squid, 27 feet (8 metres) long, hangs in the entrance hall.

Bermuda once depended on another sea creature, larger and heavier. In the late eighteenth century, whaling was an important industry and whalers set off from West Whale Bay in Southhampton Parish for their dangerous plunder of blubber. Remarkably, these massive creatures survived the bloody trade. Today, pods of migrating humpback whales, some 45 feet (14 metres) long and weighing 40 tons, can be spotted travelling through the protected waters of Bermuda's southern shores past some of the finest pink-sand beaches in the world.

Tiny, single-celled animals called Foraminifera are responsible for tinting the sand (including golf-course sand traps) this famous hue. Foraminifera grow in profusion on the underside of Bermuda's coral reefs and are pummelled by the waves into particularly fine talc sand along with shells, pieces of coral and the remains of other marine invertebrates. While coral reefs are common further south in the Caribbean, it's rare to find coral at this longitude and latitude. Bermuda's unique climate, both under and above water, is a direct result of the Gulf Stream, which brings warm water into the region, warming the air and affecting Bermuda's flora and fauna.

South Shore Park, with its 23 separate beaches all linked by walkways, offers pure, unadulterated Nirvana, miraculously free of commercial clutter. You can hike barefoot for miles along one sandy beach after another, from the long, vast Horseshoe,

Like so many things in Bermuda, the golf clubs are world-class.

Warwick Long or Elbow Bays to short and sweet beaches set inside quiet coves such as Jobson's Cove. Pad past tidal rock pools, where the air is thick with the scent of Sargasso seaweed, then crisscross over undulating dunes and grasslands dotted with campers' tents, heron nests and darting longtails. The path leads over craggy, rocky outcroppings that spy over secret coves, the water a sparkling emerald green.

Bermuda's coastline is shaped by sand and porous, grey-black limestone moulded into natural arches, caves, and freestanding statuesque forms by the pounding surf. Unlike the Caribbean, where palms frame the ocean, evergreens or deciduous trees are more common here. Before 1943, the dense, blue-green foliage of Bermuda cedar blanketed the island, its wood prized for shipbuilding, houses, furniture and fuel. By the late 1950s, however, it was wiped out by a blight. Many locals regarded this devastation as akin to losing a family member, and a replanting campaign began in earnest in the 1960s. Brides and grooms distributed a cedar seedling to all their guests, urging everyone to plant a future generation in their

honour. At the same time, tall, sturdy casuarina trees from Australia were introduced, planted in groups as windbreaks.

The long, needle-like leaves of this tropical tree whistle in high winds, an attribute golfers may not appreciate as they prepare for a tough shot, yet casuarina are commonly found on the links. Like so many things in Bermuda, the golf clubs are world-class. Designed by titans such as Robert Trent Jones, frequented by Britain's royal family and rated as some of the best in the world, the only drawback is the high cost of the game and the exclusivity of the private courses. Fortunately, challenging public courses are also available, including Horizons, Port Royal Golf Course and the Fairmont Southampton Golf Course.

The Fairmont Hotel presides over the top of a hill, a towering mammoth of pink with some 600 rooms, each offering a view of the harbour, beach and winding, three-par golf courses below. It's also home to one of Bermuda's finest French restaurants, the Newport Room, providing all the ambience of a royal yacht – shiny brass, luxuriant mahogany and uniformed staff – without

... white-washed, stepped roofs that show real ingenuity, with their grooved canals tunnelling across the surface to catch rain water and funnel it into underground tanks.

the waves. Expect seasonal, organic menu items from around the world, such as seared Quebec foie gras, Australian lamb tenderloin and artisanal cheeses from Tuscany.

Little of the food served in Bermuda is locally grown and the island depends heavily on imported food, mostly from the United States. From 1890 to 1910, Bermuda enjoyed a brief agricultural heyday with its celebrated Bermuda onion. But the onion was never trademarked, opening the door for Texan sweet-onion farmers to eliminate Bermuda as a major grower by 1920. Regardless, locals are still happy to go by the moniker 'Onion' in tribute to the days when the bulb was the best thing Bermuda had to offer. While you won't find it listed on menus, many traditional Bermudian dishes contain sweet onions, including must-taste fish chowder, garnished with a dash of Gosling's Bermuda Black rum and sherry peppers. Cassava pie is a heavy, calorie-laden dish served traditionally at Christmas, containing more than a dozen eggs, a whole chicken and lots of pork, and bound with cassava flour. On the lighter side, but not for the timid, is codfish breakfast, served on New Year's morning and featuring

salt cod and potatoes in a creamy egg or tomato sauce, along with bananas drizzled in olive oil and sliced avocado.

To protect perishable pantry items from the searing hot summers centuries ago, the Bermudians constructed a buttery, a minaret-shaped building separated from the main house. Today, the structures are used as beach houses or studio apartments. But it's Bermuda's sloping, white-washed, stepped roofs that show real ingenuity, with their grooved canals tunnelling across the surface to catch rain water and funnel it into underground tanks. Moreover, the lime wash is a natural purifier, helping to neutralize the pH in acid rain. Every home in Bermuda has a roof like this and an underground tank beneath, because there's no public water system. Old timers placed a goldfish in the tank to keep mosquitoes away.

Some of the island's oldest and most compelling architecture can be found in St George's, a UNESCO World Heritage Site since 2000 and the colony's historic heartland. At King's Square, beside the harbour and berthed cruise ships, a historic re-enactment is

A town crier officiates with
a loud bell and call.

held daily at the height of the season for the benefit of tourists. A town crier officiates with a loud bell and call, after which a token wench is dragged out, berated for lollygagging and gossiping and eventually plunged into the ocean in a dunking chair. It's an entertaining introduction to this tiny, charming and very walkable town that pulses with seventeenth- and eighteenth-century history.

The settlers who founded St George's in 1615 created a basic grid pattern that remains unchanged. The narrow lanes were designed for horse and carriage and many retain their original names, from Printer's Alley to Aunt Peggy's Lane. Historic 'firsts' abound, such as Bridge House on King Street, the island's oldest inhabited structure. Nearby St Peter's Church, on Duke of York Street, is the oldest Anglican church outside Britain, open since 1612. Its interior is rich with the cigar-box fragrance of cedar. The cemetery behind the church is a captivating blend of tended horticulture and clues to Bermuda's past. Plots on the west side are relegated to blacks and slaves. On the east, among small decaying boulders and huge, cumbersome vaults, lies the tombstone of Governor and Commander-in-Chief Sir Richard Sharples, assassinated in 1973 during a rocky, racial blip in Bermuda's recent past.

Ups and downs are the makings of any nation, let alone a 22-mile stretch of islands stranded in the North Atlantic with a history shaped by the military worth both Britain and America placed on its geography. Today, Bermuda brims with accolades, breaking all records as a business force, spilling over with historical importance, yet keeping a watchful eye over its fastidious appearance and natural beauty. So what if people confuse this island with the Caribbean. Spending even a little time in Bermuda will wash away any confusion and create a thirst to know it a lot better.

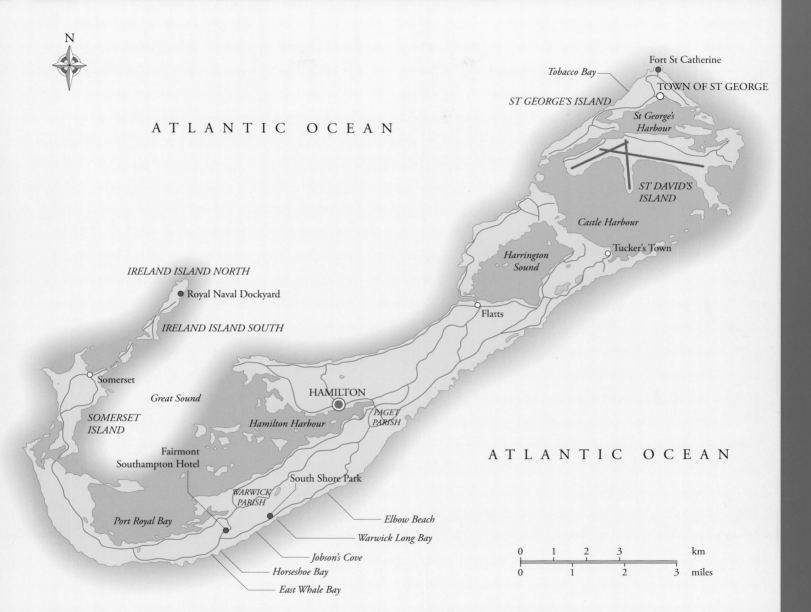

N

ATLANTIC OCEAN

Fort St Catherine

Tobacco Bay

TOWN OF ST GEORGE

ST GEORGE'S ISLAND

St George's Harbour

ST DAVID'S ISLAND

Castle Harbour

IRELAND ISLAND NORTH

Royal Naval Dockyard

IRELAND ISLAND SOUTH

Harrington Sound

Tucker's Town

Flatts

Somerset

Great Sound

SOMERSET ISLAND

HAMILTON

PAGET PARISH

Hamilton Harbour

ATLANTIC OCEAN

Fairmont Southampton Hotel

South Shore Park

WARWICK PARISH

Port Royal Bay

Elbow Beach

Warwick Long Bay

Jobson's Cove

Horseshoe Bay

East Whale Bay

| 0 | 1 | 2 | 3 | km |
| 0 | 1 | 2 | 3 | miles |

Bermuda

beaches

The clear, blue-green waters of Jobson's Cove are calm and serene. Shallow in most places and with a sandy bottom, it's perfect for kids just learning to snorkel.

The pink sands shimmer at Jobson's Cove. This intimate swimming hole is enclosed by cliffs that protect it from the open sea, forming a natural pool.

On the South Shore, beaches are framed by rocky outcroppings at either end.

Spectacular, turquoise-coloured waters on the east end of the island.

A footpath crosses over dunes and into Warwick Long Bay.
Above the beach, the rocky bluffs are a maze of paths.

A weathered jetty overlooking an impossibly azure-coloured sea near Fort St Catherine beach.

Horseshoe Bay is the most popular beach in Bermuda and crowds throng to it on summer weekends.

The bluff overlooking Fort St Catherine beach is crowned by a fort.

Warwick Long Bay is Bermuda's longest beach, with half a mile (1 km) of uninterrupted pink sand. It's the most easterly beach of the South Shore Park.

Some of the wildest rock formations on the South Shore surround Jobson's Cove.

Pounding surf on the South Shore.

The topography around St George's is shaped like a foot – hence, Achilles Bay. Situated close to Fort St Catherine, the bay is a local gem, albeit a rather small one.

A pathway connects East Whale Bay to the public beach on Horseshoe Bay.

East Whale Bay on the South Shore is a private enclave for guests staying at the Fairmont Southampton.

Looking down from a bluff above 'The Reefs' private beach.

Survivors of Sir George Somers's ship, the *Sea Venture*, called this place Tobacco Bay. It was here that Bermudians supplied the American Revolutionary War with much-needed ammunition during the Bermuda Gunpowder Plot of 1775.

A gorgeous strand of pink-sand beach on the South Shore.

The idyllic sandy cove that is Achilles Bay is normally a quiet place, although beach umbrellas and chairs are available.

The South Shore beaches are fringed with greenery.

The roaring surf on the eastern end of the island.

Warwick Long Bay is normally exposed to gusts from the south. Luckily, the surf is generally moderate here because of the protecting reefs.

Horseshoe Bay is the most popular beach in Bermuda. You can rent sun umbrellas, or do as the locals do – bring your own.

The western end of Horseshoe Bay provides a calm area popular with children.

Horsing around at Jobson's Cove.

These phantasmagorical rock formations at Tobacco Bay are created from sea-carved limestone.

architecture

Graceful allamanda are found throughout Bermuda.

Paget Parish lights up with colourful dwellings.

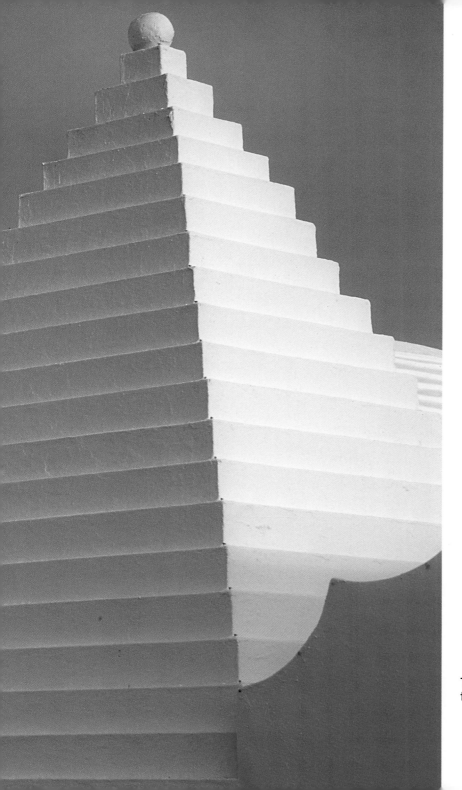

These modern and abstract whitewashed shapes all blend together perfectly in Bermuda.

The beauty of this opened, louvred window
in St George's contrasts with the flat,
whitewashed walls that are so typical here.

The whitewashed chimney and roof stand out in this classic
design found in St George's.

This cleverly designed cottage at the Elbow Beach Hotel entranceway includes an assortment of classical Bermudian architectural motifs found throughout the island.

A restored warehouse across from Hunter's Wharf, St George's.

This old Bermudian cottage is in Sandy's Parish next to the Somerset drawbridge.

Unusual latticework frames the entrance to this Paget Parish house.

This classic design is incorporated into one of the
Pink Beach Club cottages, in Tucker's Town.

Another uniquely designed Paget cottage.

Colour is used whimsically on this gated cottage found on the main road leading into St George's.

These buildings and rooflines of St George's
are all about shape, angles and colour.

Hamilton Harbour peeks out from between
two Paget cottages.

Geometric shapes are the key to classic Bermuda architecture.

A typical example of a roof formed
by overlapping Bermuda stone.

A unique home on Printer's Alley in St George's.

Historic St George's, where the colourful louvres compete for attention with the whitewashed turrets.

The Stamp House (c.1705) on the South Shore Road.

St George's

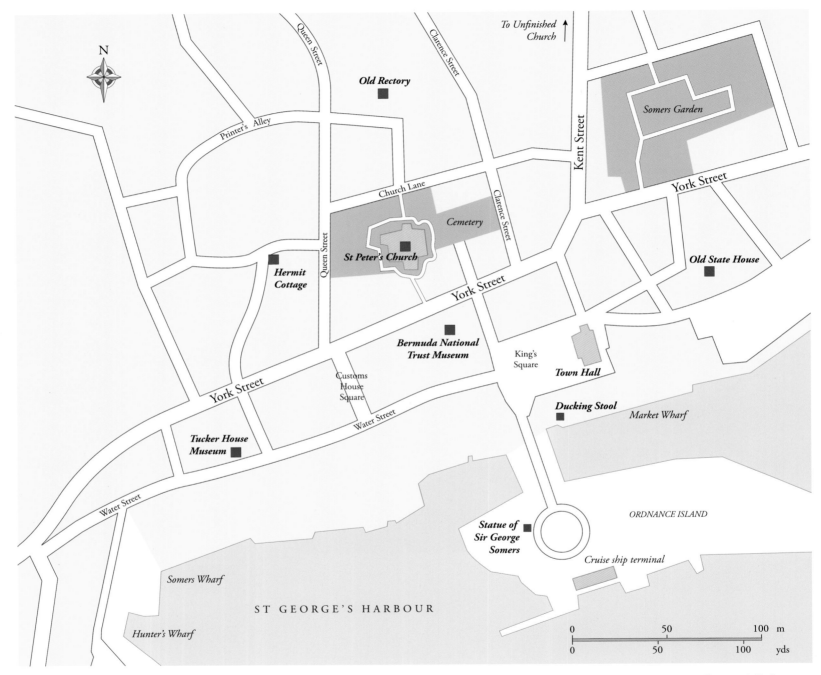

Town of St George

Public buildings in St George's near King's Square.

Colourful hibiscus flowers grow in abundance across the island.

The narrow laneways throughout St George's were originally sized for horse and carriage.

Looking down Water Street.

A colourful colonial building on Water Street which houses a motor scooter rental shop. As automobiles are not available to rent on the island, scooters have become a necessity.

A view through ironwork at the rear of the Old State House.

Water Street is popular because it's closed to traffic, becoming a pedestrian promenade during daytime hours.

The Old State House is the oldest building in Bermuda, constructed from limestone in 1620 and held together by mortar made from a mixture of turtle oil and lime. The Old State House was also used as Bermuda's Parliament, until the capital moved to Hamilton in 1815. The building has been leased to the Freemasons ever since – the rent still rankles with locals – for one peppercorn annually.

Shinbone Alley is one of the oldest passages in St George's.

A leisurely tour by horse and cart along the main thoroughfare in St George's passes by striking examples of local architecture.

King's Square is at the centre of town. There's a cannon, cenotaph and reproduction of the original pillory and stocks.

The comical and somewhat historical re-enactment of a good old-fashioned harbour-dunking is played out for the enjoyment of tourists, who are encouraged to play along as 'townsfolk'. Once the town crier has laid out the charges, the townsfolk eagerly assist in getting the accused into the ocean, via the dunking chair.

History is brought to life with town criers re-enacting moments of Bermuda's past.

Pilot Darrell's house (c.1795) is now called Hermit Cottage. This former slave was granted freedom in recognition of his ship-piloting skills. He was one of the first black Bermudians to own his own property.

In 1782, the House of Assembly set aside £450 to buy a printing press. After importing the press, the government arranged for newspaper editor John Stockdale to move to Bermuda. In 1784, the first issue of the *Bermuda Gazette* was published. John Stockdale lived in this historic home, located on Printer's Alley, until his death in 1803.

The main roadway passing through St George's is York Street.
Queen Street, once a dirt path, intersects with it. There's barely
enough room for a small car to navigate this narrow road as it
wends its way through town.

Looking across St George's Harbour to St David's Island. Many old Bermudian families still reside on the island, which is home to the airport and a former US Army base.

A cannon guards the harbour entrance to man-made Ordnance Island, which serves as a cruise ship terminal and is connected to St George's by a short causeway.

Wainwright House, a classic home on Printer's Alley, has been turned into a unique, one-bedroom B & B with majestic views of the harbour.

A rooftop view of sturdy homes all constructed from Bermuda stone on the town side of St George's harbour.

Hamilton

Just across from the ferry terminal sits the Birdcage (designed by a certain Mr Bird, no less). With its skinny metal posts and tin roof, the Birdcage is smack in the middle of a busy intersection and manned by a traffic-directing policeman during the tourist season.

Front Street is lined with Victorian buildings, and is filled with shops at street level and restaurants in the verandahs above.

Ironwork lining Front Street in front of the stately nineteenth-century Cabinet Building.

A shop along the main strip on Front Street.

Bermuda Cathedral is aptly located on Church Street. The imposing neo-Gothic structure is an Anglican church designed by Scottish architect William Hay. Work began in 1886 and was completed in 1911. A climb up the tower's 157 steps is rewarded by sweeping vistas of Hamilton.

This modern, blindingly white structure on Church Street is the City Hall. The 91-foot (28-metre) tower is adorned with a weathervane that depicts Sir George Somers's shipwrecked boat, *Sea Venture*. The interior houses Bermuda National Gallery's collection of paintings.

Sunrise on Hamilton Harbour.

A view of downtown Hamilton.

Colonial architecture lines Front Street.

The Bermuda equivalent of the British House of Commons, the House of Assembly meets in Sessions House. Built with Italian flare in 1819, it had a clock tower added in 1887 to commemorate Queen Victoria's golden jubilee. It is the third oldest parliament in the world (following those of Iceland and England). Bermuda's first parliamentary session was held in 1620 in St David's Church in St George's.

Period décor fills the rooms at the restored eighteenth-century manor house called Waterloo House, a stately hotel property that maintains the colonial tradition of high tea.

Bermuda-based Gosling Brothers Ltd. first imported barrels of Caribbean rum into Bermuda in 1860, adding their signature flavour to it. For the first 50 years of production, it was sold as draught. After World War I, the company used empty champagne bottles recovered from a British officers' mess, sealing the bottles with a black wax, leading to the brand name: Black Seal Rum.

This cenotaph is a World War 1 monument in honour of Bermuda's soldiers. Constructed in 1920 from Bermuda limestone, it's a replica of the cenotaph that stands in Whitehall, London.

Front Street shops.

Upmarket restaurants line Chancellery Lane, a charming walkway connecting Front and Church Streets.

The view along Church Street from the
Bermuda Cathedral tower.

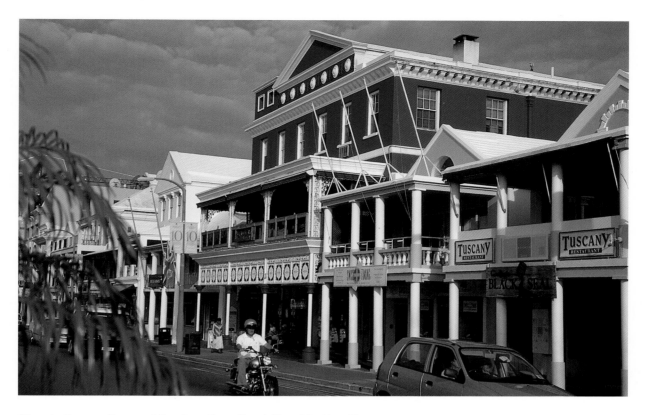

Classic Bermudian architecture lines Front Street in Hamilton.

Hamilton Harbour.

Horse and carriage is a time-honoured mode of transportation, now catering to weddings and tours around town.

'Cycles' (i.e. scooters) offer a popular way to get around.

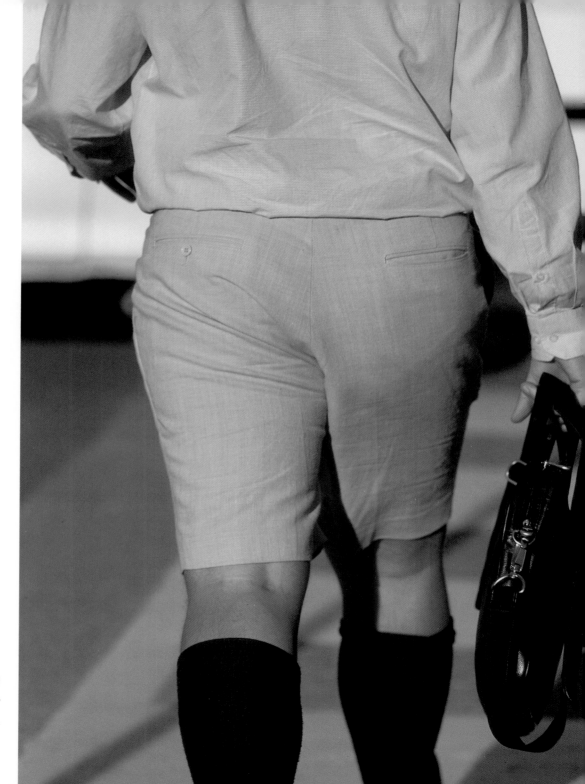

British soldiers stationed in India introduced short pants as standard military garb to Bermuda.

Two symbols of the Empire.

Despite a one-car-per-residence law, Bermuda suffers from too much traffic. Hamilton during rush hour.

Rain or shine, each weekday morning retired bus driver Johnny Barnes stands in the middle of Crow Lane roundabout and says a cheery 'Good morning!' or 'I love you!' to occupants of passing vehicles. As regular as clockwork, he's always there with his radio, backpack, straw hat and the odd souvenir for visitors.

Lunchtime sees crowds on Reid Street.

Bermuda shorts, arguably Bermuda's national costume, were introduced to the island in the early twentieth century by the British military. They are typically worn from April to November. Any haberdasher worth his salt knows these shorts hang three inches above the knee and should be worn with a blazer, tie, and high knee socks. Shorts are typically seen in a variety of colours – red, green and yellow – but also conservative grey.

Historic Bermuda

The graveyard at St Peter's Church, St George's.

St Peter's Church is the oldest Anglican church in continual use outside Britain. The original church was built in 1612 with a palmetto-thatch roof. Most of the present structure dates from 1713 but some features, such as the steeple, were later additions.

St Peter's church tower provides a 360-degree panorama of St George's. (Unfortunately, the tower is not open to the public.)

The churchyard of St Peter's was separated into two distinct graveyards: the walled area to the west of the church was reserved for black slaves, while the one on the eastern side was kept for white parishioners.

Fort Hamilton commands a spectacular vista overlooking the city of Hamilton. It was built in the 1870s to protect the city against American forces. Moats, gun emplacements and ramparts are all part of the pentagonal design.

Cedar doors and ornate doorknocker at St Peter's.

Somerset Bridge was originally built in 1620 to connect the main island to Somerset Island.
It's the shortest drawbridge in the world – just wide enough to allow a mast through.

Tucker House Museum on Water Street in St George's is currently owned by the Bermuda National Trust. It was built in the mid-eighteenth century as a merchant's house by Henry Tucker, who was also the island's colonial secretary. The antique furnishings seen today were donated by his descendants and offer a glimpse into a bygone era.

In 1874, construction commenced on the Unfinished Church. It was to replace St Peter's Church, but discord among the congregation and a lack of funds caused the project to be abandoned. It now stands as an intriguing hollow shell.

The towering red-and-white St David's lighthouse offers panoramic views, making the tiring trek up the winding wooden staircase well worth it.

This classic English phone box at Royal Naval Dockyard is still in use.

With the loss of the American colonies, the British decided to build a modern naval fortress. It was a huge task, including breakwaters, wharfs, boat slips, workshops, a victualling yard and barracks, initiated in 1809 – on the backs of thousands of convicts and slaves. The dockyards were in continual use until the 1950s.

The Royal Naval Dockyard provided an important supply station for ships sailing between Canada, the West Indies and Britain. In 1814, it was the base from which British forces invaded Washington, DC.

Bermuda's largest fort, the Keep, was constructed to defend the Royal Navy Dockyard. It is a fort within a fortress, protected by massive bastions. Its numerous cannons point out to the azure waters, aimed at an enemy that never came.

The Keep at the Royal Naval Dockyard has
30-foot (9-metre) high walls and a moat.

A warehouse located in the Great Western Storehouse complex of the Royal Naval Dockyard was completed in 1857. The chief engineer of the Dockyard had his office here.

This structure was divided into five sections: the rigger's shop, boat repair shed, cable testing house, timber store and cooperage. Many of these buildings now attract tourists, and offer displays of a variety of crafts including glass blowing and pottery.

The administrative headquarters of the Royal Navy was stationed here until the closing of the dockyards. Now it's a shopping centre. The Clocktower Mall, restored with upmarket shops, is full of activity when cruise ships are docked nearby.

The high-water clock face of the 100-foot (30-metre) eastern tower of the Clocktower was installed to let mariners know the time of high tide.

The Clocktower Mall's western tower
continues to tell the correct time.

Stamp House (c.1705) is found on
South Shore Road in Warwick Parish.

A small battery of cannons adorns the fortifications at
Gates Fort. The strategic location of the lookout tower
provided a bird's-eye view of ship traffic navigating the cut,
a narrow channel that leads into St George's Harbour.

Desmond Fountain sculpted the statue of Sir George Somers which stands on tiny Ordnance Island a stone's throw from King's Square in St George's.

Constructed prior to 1700 by reformed pirate and slave trader George Dew, the Old Rectory is one of the oldest buildings in St George's. It's located on Broad Alley, behind St Peter's Church. Although it's a historic site owned by the Bermuda National Trust, two rooms are available for Bed & Breakfast. The public can tour the house with its antique furnishings and colonial charm, in the winter months only.

The exhibitions at the Bermuda National Trust Museum, St George's, outline Bermuda's role in the American Civil War. Speedy steamships from the Southern states would run the Union blockades and unload their cargo here – mainly cotton headed for mills in England. Once in Bermuda, it would be transferred to ships heading for England in exchange for materials needed for the war effort in the Southern states. Many Bermuda merchants made a fortune through blockade running.

The Bermuda National Trust Museum is housed in one of Bermuda's oldest stone buildings. Built around 1700 by Governor Samuel Day, it was originally used as his residence. At some point in the mid-nineteenth century it was the site of the Globe Hotel, later housing agents of the Confederate Government.

Carter House, built in the 1640s, is believed to be one of the oldest buildings in Bermuda. It was built by descendants of Christopher Carter, who came to the island on the ill-fated *Sea Venture*, which foundered here in 1609. Located on St David's Island, Carter House is situated on the former site of the US military base.

Exposed timber beams and a Union Jack are highlights of St Peter's Church, which has been in use since 1625 and was built by Bermuda's first governor, Richard Moore, in 1615. The historic altar remains from the original structure and is the oldest example of Bermudian woodwork known to exist.

In 1612, Bermuda's first governor, Richard Moore, arrived from England with 60 settlers aboard the *Plough*. Moore, a carpenter by trade, built a wooden fort – Fort St Catherine – to defend Bermuda from the Spaniards. It was built upon a hill above a beautiful beach and rebuilt several times. The most recent structure dates back to the late nineteenth century.

Little has changed at Tucker House, St George's, since the days of Henry Tucker in the eighteenth century. Portraits of Tucker family members adorn the walls, and original mahogany and cedar furnishings fill the rooms.